My Bilingual Picture Book

Mon album illustré bilingue

Sefa's most beautiful children's stories in one volume

Ulrich Renz • Barbara Brinkmann:

Sleep Tight, Little Wolf · Dors bien, petit loup

For ages 2 and up

Cornelia Haas • Ulrich Renz:

My Most Beautiful Dream · Mon plus beau rêve

For ages 2 and up

Ulrich Renz • Marc Robitzky:

The Wild Swans · Les cygnes sauvages

Based on a fairy tale by Hans Christian Andersen

For ages 5 and up

© 2024 by Sefa Verlag Kirsten Bödeker, Lübeck, Germany. www.sefa-verlag.de

Special thanks to Paul Bödeker, Freiburg, Germany

All rights reserved.

ISBN: 9783756304332

Read · Listen · Understand

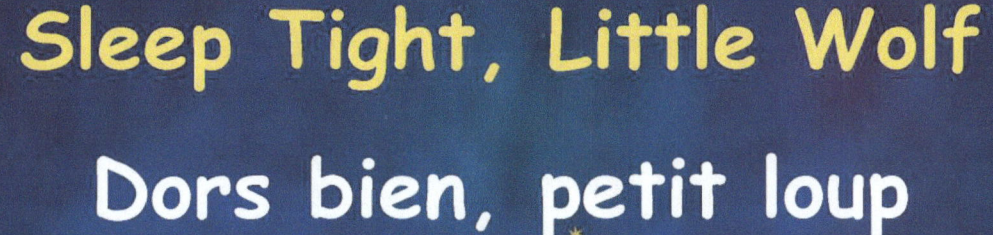

Translation:

Pete Savill (English)

Céleste Lottigier (French)

Audiobook and video:

www.sefa-bilingual.com/bonus

Password for free access:

English: `LWEN1423`

French: `LWFR1527`

Good night, Tim! We'll continue searching tomorrow.
Now sleep tight!

Bonne nuit, Tim ! On continuera à chercher demain.
Dors bien maintenant !

It is already dark outside.

Dehors, il fait déjà nuit.

What is Tim doing?

Mais que fait Tim là ?

He is leaving for the playground.
What is he looking for there?

Il va dehors, à l'aire de jeu.
Qu'est-ce qu'il y cherche ?

The little wolf!

He can't sleep without it.

Le petit loup !

Sans lui, il ne peut pas dormir.

Who's this coming?

Mais qui arrive là ?

Marie! She's looking for her ball.

Marie ! Elle cherche son ballon.

And what is Tobi looking for?

Et Tobi, qu'est-ce qu'il cherche ?

His digger.

Sa pelleteuse.

And what is Nala looking for?

Et Nala, qu'est-ce qu'elle cherche ?

Her doll.

Sa poupée.

Don't the children have to go to bed?

The cat is rather surprised.

Les enfants ne doivent-ils pas aller au lit ?

Le chat est très surpris.

Who's coming now?

Qui vient donc là ?

Tim's mum and dad!

They can't sleep without their Tim.

Le papa et la maman de Tim !

Sans leur Tim, ils ne peuvent pas dormir.

More of them are coming! Marie's dad.
Tobi's grandpa. And Nala's mum.

Et en voilà encore d'autres qui arrivent !
Le papa de Marie. Le papi de Tobi. Et la maman de Nala.

Now hurry to bed everyone!

Vite au lit maintenant !

Good night, Tim!
Tomorrow we won't have to search any longer.

Bonne nuit, Tim !
Demain nous n'aurons plus besoin de chercher.

Sleep tight, little wolf!

Dors bien, petit loup !

Cornelia Haas • Ulrich Renz

My Most Beautiful Dream

Mon plus beau rêve

Translation:

Sefâ Jesse Konuk Agnew (English)

Martin Andler (French)

Audiobook and video:

www.sefa-bilingual.com/bonus

Password for free access:

English: **BDEN1423**

French: **BDFR1527**

My Most Beautiful Dream
Mon plus beau rêve

Cornelia Haas · Ulrich Renz

English — bilingual — French

Lulu can't fall asleep. Everyone else is dreaming already – the shark, the elephant, the little mouse, the dragon, the kangaroo, the knight, the monkey, the pilot. And the lion cub. Even the bear has trouble keeping his eyes open …

Hey bear, will you take me along into your dream?

Lulu n'arrive pas à s'endormir. Tous les autres rêvent déjà – le requin, l'éléphant, la petite souris, le dragon, le kangourou, le chevalier, le singe, le pilote. Et le bébé lion. Même Nounours a du mal à garder ses yeux ouverts.

Eh Nounours, tu m'emmènes dans ton rêve ?

And with that, Lulu finds herself in bear dreamland. The bear catches fish in Lake Tagayumi. And Lulu wonders, who could be living up there in the trees?

When the dream is over, Lulu wants to go on another adventure. Come along, let's visit the shark! What could he be dreaming?

Tout de suite, voilà Lulu dans le pays des rêves des ours. Nounours attrape des poissons dans le lac Tagayumi. Et Lulu se demande qui peut bien vivre là-haut dans les arbres ?

Quand le rêve est fini, Lulu veut encore une aventure. Viens avec moi, allons voir le requin ! De quoi peut-il bien rêver ?

The shark plays tag with the fish. Finally he's got some friends! Nobody's afraid of his sharp teeth.

When the dream is over, Lulu wants to go on another adventure. Come along, let's visit the elephant! What could he be dreaming?

Le requin joue à chat avec les poissons. Enfin, il a des amis ! Personne n'a peur de ses dents pointues.

Quand le rêve est fini, Lulu veut encore une aventure. Venez avec moi, allons voir l'éléphant ! De quoi peut-il bien rêver ?

The elephant is as light as a feather and can fly! He's about to land on the celestial meadow.

When the dream is over, Lulu wants to go on another adventure. Come along, let's visit the little mouse! What could she be dreaming?

L'éléphant est léger comme une plume et il peut voler ! Dans un instant il va se poser dans la prairie céleste.
Quand le rêve est fini, Lulu veut encore une aventure. Venez avec moi, allons voir la petite souris. De quoi peut-elle bien rêver ?

The little mouse watches the fair. She likes the roller coaster best. When the dream is over, Lulu wants to go on another adventure. Come along, let's visit the dragon! What could she be dreaming?

La petite souris visite la fête foraine. Ce qui lui plaît le plus, ce sont les montagnes russes.
Quand le rêve est fini, Lulu veut encore une aventure. Venez avec moi, allons voir le dragon. De quoi peut-il bien rêver ?

The dragon is thirsty from spitting fire. She'd like to drink up the whole lemonade lake.

When the dream is over, Lulu wants to go on another adventure. Come along, let's visit the kangaroo! What could she be dreaming?

Le dragon a soif à force de cracher le feu. Il voudrait boire tout le lac de limonade !

Quand le rêve est fini, Lulu veut encore une aventure. Venez avec moi, allons voir le kangourou. De quoi peut-il bien rêver ?

The kangaroo jumps around the candy factory and fills her pouch. Even more of the blue sweets! And more lollipops! And chocolate!
When the dream is over, Lulu wants to go on another adventure. Come along, let's visit the knight! What could he be dreaming?

Le kangourou sautille dans la fabrique de bonbons et remplit sa poche. Encore plus de ces bonbons bleus ! Et plus de sucettes ! Et du chocolat ! Quand le rêve est fini, Lulu veut encore une aventure. Venez avec moi, allons voir le chevalier ! De quoi peut-il bien rêver ?

The knight is having a cake fight with his dream princess. Oops! The whipped cream cake has gone the wrong way!
When the dream is over, Lulu wants to go on another adventure. Come along, let's visit the monkey! What could he be dreaming?

Le chevalier a une bataille de gâteaux avec la princesse de ses rêves. Ouh-la-la, le gâteau à la crème a râté son but !

Quand le rêve est fini, Lulu veut encore une aventure. Venez avec moi, allons voir le singe ! De quoi peut-il bien rêver ?

Snow has finally fallen in Monkeyland. The whole barrel of monkeys is beside itself and getting up to monkey business.
When the dream is over, Lulu wants to go on another adventure. Come along, let's visit the pilot! In which dream could he have landed?

Il a enfin neigé au pays des singes. Toute leur bande est en folie, et fait des bêtises.

Quand le rêve est fini, Lulu veut encore une aventure. Venez avec moi, allons voir le pilote ! Sur quel rêve a-t-il pu se poser ?

The pilot flies on and on. To the ends of the earth, and even farther, right on up to the stars. No other pilot has ever managed that.
When the dream is over, everybody is very tired and doesn't feel like going on many adventures anymore. But they'd still like to visit the lion cub.
What could she be dreaming?

Le pilote vole et vole. Jusqu'au bout du monde, et encore au delà, jusqu'aux étoiles. Jamais aucun pilote ne l'avait fait.
Quand le rêve est fini, ils sont déjà tous très fatigués, et n'ont plus trop envie d'aventures. Mais quand même, ils veulent encore voir le bébé lion.
De quoi peut-il bien rêver ?

The lion cub is homesick and wants to go back to the warm, cozy bed.
And so do the others.

And thus begins ...

Le bébé lion a le mal du pays, et voudrait retourner dans son lit bien chaud et douillet.
Et les autres aussi.

Et voilà que commence ...

... Lulu's
most beautiful dream.

... le plus beau rêve
de Lulu.

Ulrich Renz • Marc Robitzky

The Wild Swans

Les cygnes sauvages

Translation:

Ludwig Blohm, Pete Savill (English)

Martin Andler (French)

Audiobook and video:

www.sefa-bilingual.com/bonus

Password for free access:

English: **WSEN1423**

French: **WSFR1527**

Ulrich Renz · Marc Robitzky

The Wild Swans

Les cygnes sauvages

Based on a fairy tale by

Hans Christian Andersen

+ audio   + video

English   bilingual   **French**

Once upon a time there were twelve royal children – eleven brothers and one older sister, Elisa. They lived happily in a beautiful castle.

Il était une fois douze enfants royaux — onze frères et une sœur ainée, Elisa. Ils vivaient heureux dans un magnifique château.

One day the mother died, and some time later the king married again. The new wife, however, was an evil witch. She turned the eleven princes into swans and sent them far away to a distant land beyond the large forest.

Un jour, la mère mourut, et après un certain temps, le roi se remaria. Mais la nouvelle épouse était une méchante sorcière. Elle changea les onze princes en cygnes et les envoya dans un pays éloigné, au delà de la grande forêt.

She dressed the girl in rags and smeared an ointment onto her face that turned her so ugly, that even her own father no longer recognized her and chased her out of the castle. Elisa ran into the dark forest.

Elle habilla la fille de haillons et enduisit son visage d'une pommade répugnante, si bien que son propre père ne la reconnut pas et la chassa du château. Elisa courut vers la sombre forêt.

Now she was all alone, and longed for her missing brothers from the depths of her soul. As the evening came, she made herself a bed of moss under the trees.

Elle était alors toute seule et ses frères lui manquaient terriblement au plus profond de son âme. Quand le soir vint, elle se confectionna un lit de mousse sous les arbres.

The next morning she came to a calm lake and was shocked when she saw her reflection in it. But once she had washed, she was the most beautiful princess under the sun.

Le lendemain matin, elle arriva à un lac tranquille et fut choquée de voir son reflet dans l'eau. Une fois lavée, cependant, elle redevint le plus bel enfant royal sous le soleil.

After many days Elisa reached the great sea. Eleven swan feathers were bobbing on the waves.

Après de nombreux jours, elle arriva à la grande mer. Sur les vagues dansaient onze plumes de cygnes.

As the sun set, there was a swooshing noise in the air and eleven wild swans landed on the water. Elisa immediately recognized her enchanted brothers. They spoke swan language and because of this she could not understand them.

Au coucher du soleil, il y eut un bruissement dans l'air, et onze cygnes sauvages se posèrent sur l'eau. Elisa reconnut tout de suite ses frères ensorcelés. Mais comme ils parlaient la langue des cygnes, elle ne pouvait pas les comprendre.

During the day the swans flew away, and at night the siblings snuggled up together in a cave.

One night Elisa had a strange dream: Her mother told her how she could release her brothers from the spell. She should knit shirts from stinging nettles and throw one over each of the swans. Until then, however, she was not allowed to speak a word, or else her brothers would die.
Elisa set to work immediately. Although her hands were burning as if they were on fire, she carried on knitting tirelessly.

Chaque jour, les cygnes s'envolaient au loin, et la nuit, les frères et sœurs se blottissaient les uns contre les autres dans une grotte.

Une nuit, Elisa fit un rêve étrange : sa mère lui disait comment racheter ses frères. Elle devrait tricoter une chemise d'orties à chacun des cygnes et les leur jeter dessus. Mais avant d'en être là, il ne fallait pas qu'elle prononce un seul mot : sinon ses frères allaient mourir.
Elisa se mit au travail immédiatement. Et bien que ses mains lui brûlaient comme du feu, elle tricotait et tricotait inlassablement.

One day hunting horns sounded in the distance. A prince came riding along with his entourage and he soon stood in front of her. As they looked into each other's eyes, they fell in love.

Un jour, des cornes de chasse se firent entendre au loin. Un prince, accompagné de son entourage, arriva à cheval et s'arrêta devant elle. Quand leurs regards se croisèrent, ils tombèrent amoureux.

The prince lifted Elisa onto his horse and rode to his castle with her.

Le prince prit Elisa sur son cheval et l'emmena dans son château.

The mighty treasurer was anything but pleased with the arrival of the silent beauty. His own daughter was meant to become the prince's bride.

Le très puissant trésorier fut loin d'être content de l'arrivée de cette beauté muette : c'était sa fille à lui qui devait devenir la femme du prince !

Elisa had not forgotten her brothers. Every evening she continued working on the shirts. One night she went out to the cemetery to gather fresh nettles. While doing so she was secretly watched by the treasurer.

Elisa n'avait pas oublié ses frères. Chaque soir, elle poursuivait son travail sur les chemises. Une nuit, elle alla au cimetière pour cueillir des orties fraiches. Le trésorier l'observa en cachette.

As soon as the prince was away on a hunting trip, the treasurer had Elisa thrown into the dungeon. He claimed that she was a witch who met with other witches at night.

Dès que le prince partit à la chasse, le trésorier fit enfermer Elisa dans le donjon. Il prétendait qu'elle était une sorcière qui se réunissait avec d'autres sorcières la nuit.

At dawn, Elisa was fetched by the guards. She was going to be burned to death at the marketplace.

Au petit matin Elisa fut emmenée par les gardes. Elle devait être brûlée sur la place du marché.

No sooner had she arrived there, when suddenly eleven white swans came flying towards her. Elisa quickly threw a shirt over each of them. Shortly thereafter all her brothers stood before her in human form. Only the smallest, whose shirt had not been quite finished, still had a wing in place of one arm.

A peine y fut-elle arrivée qu'onze cygnes arrivèrent en volant. Elisa, très vite, jeta une chemise d'orties sur chacun d'eux. Bientôt, tous ses frères étaient devant elle en forme humaine. Seul le plus petit, dont la chemise n'était pas terminée, avait encore une aile à la place d'un bras.

The siblings' joyous hugging and kissing hadn't yet finished as the prince returned. At last Elisa could explain everything to him. The prince had the evil treasurer thrown into the dungeon. And after that the wedding was celebrated for seven days.

And they all lived happily ever after.

Les frères et la sœur étaient encore en train de s'étreindre et de s'embrasser quand le prince revint. Elisa put enfin tout lui expliquer. Le prince fit jeter le méchant trésorier dans le donjon. Après quoi, le mariage fut célébré pendant sept jours.

Et ils vécurent heureux et eurent beaucoup d'enfants.

Hans Christian Andersen

Hans Christian Andersen was born in the Danish city of Odense in 1805, and died in 1875 in Copenhagen. He gained world fame with his literary fairy-tales such as „The Little Mermaid", „The Emperor's New Clothes" and „The Ugly Duckling". The tale at hand, „The Wild Swans", was first published in 1838. It has been translated into more than one hundred languages and adapted for a wide range of media including theater, film and musical.

Barbara Brinkmann was born in Munich in 1969 and grew up in the foothills of the Bavarian Alps. She studied architecture in Munich and is currently a research associate in the Department of Architecture at the Technical University of Munich. She also works as a freelance graphic designer, illustrator, and author.

Cornelia Haas has been illustrating childrens' and adolescents' books since 2001. She was born near Augsburg, Germany, in 1972. She studied design at the Münster University of Applied Sciences and is currently a professor on the faculty of Münster University of Applied Sciences teaching illustration.

Marc Robitzky, born in 1973, studied at the Technical School of Art in Hamburg and the Academy of Visual Arts in Frankfurt. He works as a freelance illustrator and communication designer in Aschaffenburg (Germany).

Ulrich Renz was born in Stuttgart, Germany, in 1960. After studying French literature in Paris he graduated from medical school in Lübeck and worked as head of a scientific publishing company. He is now a writer of non-fiction books as well as children's fiction books.

Do you like drawing?

Here are the pictures from the story to color in:

www.sefa-bilingual.com/coloring

www.ingramcontent.com/pod-product-compliance
Lightning Source LLC
LaVergne TN
LVHW070448080526
838202LV00035B/2775